GETTING TO KNOW THE WORLD'S GREATEST INVENTORS & SCIENTISTS

MARIE CURIE

Scientist Who Made Glowing Discoveries

WRITTEN AND ILLUSTRATED BY MIKE VENEZIA

CHILDREN'S PRESS®
AN IMPRINT OF SCHOLASTIC INC.
NEW YORK TORONTO LONDON AUCKLAND SYDNEY
MEXICO CITY NEW DELHI HONG KONG
DANBURY, CONNECTICUT

W9-AOV-389

Reading Consultant: Nanci R. Vargus, Ed.D., Assistant Professor, School of Education, University of Indianapolis

Content Consultant: Joyce Bedi, Senior Historian, Lemelson Center for the Study of Invention and Innovation, National Museum of American History, Smithsonian Institution

Photographs © 2009: ACJC-Curie and Joliot Curie Archives: 16 top, 28; Alamy Images: 30 (Popperfoto), 13, 14, 31 (The Print Collector); Art Resource, NY/The Museum of Modern Art/Licensed by SCALA: 17 (Henri de Toulouse-Lautrec (1864-1901), *Mademoiselle Eglantine's Troupe*, 1896); Corbis Images: 12 (Hulton-Deutsch Collection), 24; Photo Researchers, NY: 7 (Michael Dunning), 22 (Astrid & Hans Michler/SPL), 21 (SPL), 6; The Art Archive/Picture Desk/Culver Pictures: 27; The Granger Collection, New York: 26; The Image Works: 8 (ARPL/HIP), 18 (Jacques Boyer/Roger-Viollet), 20 (Albert Harlingue/Roger-Viollet), 3, 15 (Mary Evans Picture Library), 16 bottom (Camille Pissarro, *The Boulevard Montmartre at Night*, 1897/National Gallery Collection, London/Art Media/Heritage-Images).

Colorist for illustrations: Andrew Day

Library of Congress Cataloging-in-Publication Data

Venezia, Mike.
  Marie Curie : scientist who made glowing discoveries / written and
illustrated by Mike Venezia.
      p. cm. — (Getting to know the world's greatest inventors and scientists)
  Includes index.
  ISBN 13: 978-0-531-14977-5 (lib. bdg.) 978-0-531-22208-9 (pbk.)
  ISBN 10: 0-531-14977-3 (lib. bdg.)   0-531-22208-X (pbk.)
  1. Curie, Marie, 1867-1934—Juvenile literature. 2.
Chemists—Poland—Biography—Juvenile literature. 3. Women
chemists—Poland—Biography—Juvenile literature. 4.
Chemists—France—Biography—Juvenile literature. 5. Women
chemists—France—Biography—Juvenile literature. I. Title. II. Series.

  QD22.C8V46 2008
  540.92—dc22
  [B]   2008002301

No part of this publication may be reproduced in whole or in part, or stored
in a retrieval system, or transmitted in any form or by any means, electronic,
mechanical, photocopying, recording, or otherwise, without written permission
of the publisher. For information regarding permission, write to
Scholastic Inc., 557 Broadway, New York, NY 10012.

© 2009 by Mike Venezia.

All rights reserved. Published in 2009 by Children's Press, an imprint of Scholastic Inc.
Published simultaneously in Canada. Printed in China.

SCHOLASTIC, CHILDREN'S PRESS, and associated logos are trademarks
and/or registered trademarks of Scholastic Inc.

7 8 9 10 R 18 17 16 15

Marie Curie, shown here in her laboratory in 1921, was the first woman to win a Nobel Prize.

Marie Curie was born Maria Sklodowska in Warsaw, Poland, in 1867. She changed her name to Marie when she moved to France as a young woman. When she was a little girl, Marie dreamed of becoming a scientist. When she grew up, her dream came true. In fact, she and her husband Pierre became two of the most important scientists in the world!

Marie Curie made important discoveries about the basic materials that make up the universe. In 1898, she discovered two new **elements.** She named one **polonium** and the other **radium.** Elements are materials that can't be separated into anything else. They're totally pure. Gold, **uranium,** and oxygen are examples of elements.

When Marie was born, there were only 63 known elements. Today, more than 100 elements have been discovered. Scientists are always looking for new ones, too. One thing that made polonium and radium remarkable was that they gave off mysterious and powerful invisible **rays!** These rays of energy are called **radiation.**

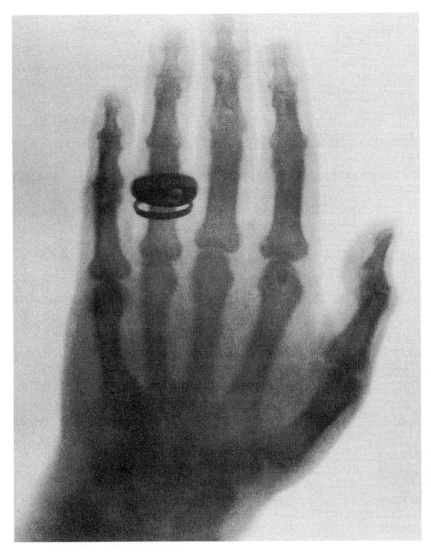

X-rays were discovered in 1895 by German scientist Wilhelm Roentgen. This is one of the world's first X-rays. The dark object on the person's hand is a ring.

One of Marie Curie's greatest accomplishments was finding out where the mysterious rays came from. Scientists already knew about X-rays and radiation, but no one was sure what caused the rays. Marie Curie believed the powerful rays from polonium and radium came from tiny **atoms** that were disintegrating inside her newly discovered elements.

Until this time, scientists believed atoms were solid and could never change. But Marie turned out to be right. She and her husband Pierre did experiments that helped unlock the secrets of the atom. Their discoveries led to new sources of energy and the beginning of the **atomic age**.

This diagram shows the structure of an atom. An atom is the tiniest part of an element that has all the properties of that element. Everything is made up of atoms. They are so small that they can be seen only by the most powerful microscopes.

There were five children in the Sklodowska family (from left to right): Zosia, Hela, Maria, Joseph, and Bronya.

For someone who wanted to be a scientist, Marie couldn't have grown up in a better family. Both her parents were teachers. They believed education was the most important thing in the world. They knew how to make learning fun, too.

All five of the Sklodowska children were brilliant students. Marie, the youngest, was the brightest of them all. Even when Marie was very young, her brother and sisters would sometimes ask her for help with their homework.

Marie never had a problem getting top grades in school. Even so, her childhood was not a happy one. In the 1800s, Poland was ruled by Russia. The Russian government treated Polish citizens, including schoolchildren, very badly. If students were caught speaking Polish instead of Russian, or studying Polish history rather than Russian history, the whole class could be arrested!

Sometimes Russian inspectors dropped in unexpectedly. Because Marie spoke Russian better than other students, she was always chosen to answer the inspector's questions.

Marie began feeling nervous and uneasy a lot of the time. When she was ten years old, things got even worse. Marie's mother died of a disease called **tuberculosis**. To get her mind off the terrible loss, Marie threw herself into her studies. Five years later, in 1883, Marie graduated high school, first in her class.

Russian troops in Warsaw in the early 1860s

Marie loved to learn. She really wanted to go to college, but there was a problem. In Poland at the time, women weren't allowed to attend any universities. Marie could have traveled to Paris, France, where women were accepted into college, but she didn't have the money for living expenses.

In the meantime, Marie attended a secret school for women. Classes were held late at night in different apartments and private homes. During this time, Marie worked out a deal with her older sister, Bronya. Marie offered to work and help pay for Bronya's medical school in Paris. Then, when Bronya graduated, she would help pay for Marie's education.

Marie (at left) and her sister Bronya in 1886

The plan worked perfectly. Marie got a well-paying job as a **governess**. She cared for and taught the children of wealthy people. Marie worked hard, saved money, and sent it to Bronya. In her spare time, Marie read and studied every book she could find on her favorite subject, science. Finally, after almost five years, Bronya graduated. She had also gotten married during this time.

When she was eighteen, Marie worked as a governess at this house in Poland.

Marie earned money taking care of children—like the governess in this illustration—while she waited for her chance to go to college.

Bronya and her husband invited Marie to come to France to enter the University of Paris. When Marie arrived in Paris, she couldn't believe her eyes. Paris was much different from anything she had ever imagined.

In the late 1800s, Paris was one of the most exciting cities in the world. People there seemed to be free to do and say whatever they wanted. Paris was filled with modern writers, poets, and Impressionist artists. It had exciting nightclubs where people enjoyed watching famous can-can dancers.

The photograph at right shows Marie in 1892, soon after she arrived in Paris. This painting by Camille Pissarro, *Boulevard Montmartre at Night*, shows what a vibrant city Paris was at the time.

In the late 1800s, Paris was an exciting city that attracted artists, writers, and scientists. This poster by famous French artist Henri de Toulouse-Lautrec shows Paris dancers of the time.

Best of all, though, women were welcome to enter the Sorbonne, another name for the University of Paris at the time. Marie couldn't wait to register. She chose courses in **physics**. Physics is the science that deals with matter and energy and how they interact. It includes the study of light, heat, sound, and motion. Marie worked as hard as she could, often studying late into the night.

After two years, Marie did something that had never been done before. She was the first woman to receive a physics degree at the Sorbonne. Not only that, but Marie was first in her class! After graduating, Marie began looking for a workspace to continue scientific experiments. Marie's search would lead to a big change in her life. Marie Sklodowska was introduced to Pierre Curie, a well-known scientist and professor.

Marie met and fell in love with Pierre Curie, a well-known French scientist. They married in 1895.

Pierre found a space in a storage shed at his school for Marie to use. Marie and Pierre soon found they had a lot in common. They began dating. The brilliant couple enjoyed spending hours talking about complicated scientific subjects. In 1895, Marie and Pierre decided to get married. They eventually had two daughters, Irène and Eve.

Marie and Pierre Curie with their daughter Irène

Their first daughter, Irène, was born in 1897. As busy as Marie was with a new baby, she was determined to continue her education. Pierre encouraged Marie to get her PhD. A PhD, or **doctorate**, is the highest degree a school can give out. To earn this degree, though, Marie needed to choose an important scientific subject to study and write a paper about.

Scientists at the time knew that uranium gives off radiation. Marie decided to try and find out if there were any other materials besides uranium that were **radioactive**. Marie also wanted to find out what caused the mysterious invisible rays that were powerful enough to pass through skin, bones, wood, and even some metals. After months of hard work, Marie discovered materials that gave off even more powerful rays than uranium does.

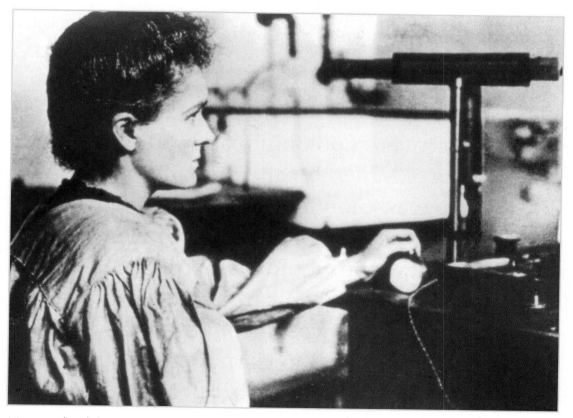

Marie in her laboratory, measuring radioactivity, in the late 1890s

Marie wanted to prove that pitchblende (right) contained other radioactive elements besides uranium.

Marie discovered polonium and radium in a mixture of minerals called **pitchblende**. Pitchblende was known to contain uranium, but no one guessed it contained other elements, too. Marie knew she would have to separate her newly discovered elements from other materials in the pitchblende. It was the only way to prove they really existed, and to learn more about each one. It wasn't an easy job, but Marie never minded hard work.

Marie had to boil tons of pitchblende in water with acid and other chemicals. She stirred the smelly mess with a heavy iron rod. Marie would then test the leftover sludge. She got rid of any material that wasn't radioactive and kept the rest. Polonium was the first new radioactive element Marie separated out. She named it after her native country, Poland.

It took Marie a few more years to separate a small amount of pure radium from pitchblende. Marie and Pierre were surprised to find that radium gave off a strange bluish-green glow. Sometimes, for fun, they would spend evenings in the laboratory watching their discovery glow in the dark.

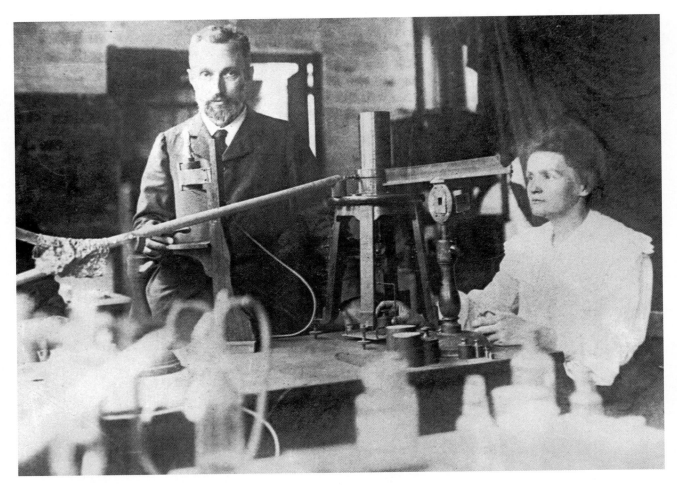

Pierre and Marie in their laboratory

Marie presented her findings to her professors at the Sorbonne. She had discovered two new elements. Marie suggested that the rays or energy they gave off were actually particles from disintegrating atoms. Eventually, scientists would prove that she had been right. Marie was awarded her doctorate degree in 1903, the first woman in France to receive the high honor.

Marie and her daughters Eve (left) and Irène are shown here in 1903. That year, Marie and Pierre Curie shared the Nobel Prize for Physics for their research on radiation.

Marie and Pierre became world famous for their discoveries and experiments on radiation. They received awards and were given money to help continue their research. Then, just when things seemed to be going great, a terrible tragedy happened.

While crossing a busy Paris street, Pierre was run down by a speeding horse-drawn wagon. He was killed instantly. A shocked Marie Curie was suddenly left alone with two young daughters. As grief-stricken as she was, Marie did her best to raise her daughters and carry on with her work.

After Pierre died in 1906, Marie continued doing research on her own. In 1911, she was the sole winner of the Nobel Prize for Chemistry.

Tho-Radia, a facial cream containing radium, was sold in the 1920s and 1930s. At the time, people didn't know about the harmful effects of radium.

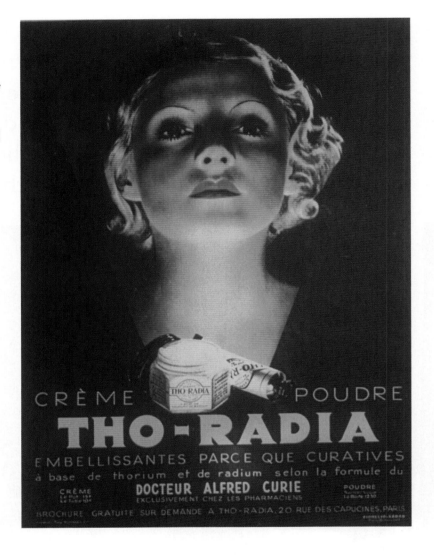

When news about the discovery of radium got around, people all over the world were curious to see what its mysterious powerful rays could do. Radium was found to be valuable in fighting cancer and other serious diseases. Radium was often misused, however.

Some manufacturers believed radium would be good for skin and hair care. They began making products that contained small amounts of radium. At the time, no one knew that radium could be very dangerous if it wasn't handled properly.

Marie's daughter Irène also became a famous scientist. As a young girl, she worked with her mother in the laboratory.

Early into their research, both Marie and Pierre began feeling like they had flu all the time. They also had strange burns on their fingers. Later, doctors would learn that the Curies had radiation poisoning. When Marie died at the age of sixty-six, it was from the effects of handling radium during years of research.

By the time she died in 1934, Marie Curie was one of the most famous scientists in the world. Throughout her career, she had generously shared her discoveries and knowledge with other scientists. She always believed in the good that science could do for people all over the world, and was willing to prove it. During World War I, Marie equipped trucks with X-ray machines and trained people to use them. Marie bravely traveled to battlefield areas to assist doctors. She helped save the lives of thousands of wounded soldiers.

During World War I, Marie Curie drove this X-ray-equipped truck from hospital to hospital to help wounded soldiers.

Glossary

atom (AT-uhm) The tiniest part of an element that has all the properties of that element; everything is made up of atoms

atomic age (uh-TOM-ik AJE) The period in history after the first use of the atomic bomb

doctorate (DOK-tur-it) The highest degree given by a university

element (EL-uh-muhnt) In chemistry, a substance that cannot be split into a smaller substance

governess (GUHV-ur-ness) A woman who cares for children in a private home

physics (FIZ-iks) The science that deals with matter and energy

pitchblende (PICH-blend) A mineral that contains radium and is the main source of uranium

polonium (puh-LONE-ee-um) A radioactive element

radiation (ray-dee-AY-shuhn) Energy or rays sent out when changes happen in the atoms of an object

radioactive (ray-dee-oh-AK-tiv) Describing materials made up of atoms that break down, giving off radiation

radium (RAY-dee-um) A radioactive element; it is sometimes used to treat cancer but in large amounts can cause cancer

ray (RAY) A narrow beam of energy

tuberculosis (tu-BUR-kyuh-LOH-siss) A contagious disease that usually affects the lungs

uranium (yoo-RAY-nee-um) A radioactive element used in producing atomic energy

Index